Ulster's Scottish Connection

Michael Hall

ISLAND (3) PAMPHLETS

Published by Island Publications
132 Serpentine Road, Newtownabey, Co Antrim

Illustration Credits:

Hugh Thomson: pages 12, 13
(from *Highways and Byways in Galloway and Carrick*, MacMillan, 1927)

Hugh Thomson: pages 8, 21, 25, 29
(from *Highways and Byways in Donegal and Antrim*, MacMillan, 1903)

Unknown: pages 14, 20, 23
(from *The History of Scotland*, Rev James Mackenzie, Nelson & Sons, 1890)

John McCloskey: pages 17, 26, 27

Robin Hall: pages 5, 11

Gary Hamilton: page 16

This publication has received financial assistance from

The Cultural Coalition;

Pretani Press

Printed by Regency Press, Belfast

Preface

The summit of the Cave Hill provides a stunning panoramic view over Belfast. There are not many cities which can be seen in their entirely from a single vantage point; nor, I imagine – looking at the matter the other way round – do many cities have such a majestic backdrop dominating their skyline. The purity of the air, the freshness of the breeze and the sheerness of the drop under the headland combine to create an exhilarating effect on the senses, and one trip to the summit is never enough.

A former work-colleague – who sadly died a few months after his retirement – used to climb to the summit whenever he felt burdened down by everyday pressures. The magnificent view from the top not only helped ease away any depressive thoughts, he informed me, but allowed him to view Belfast's share of humanity – especially those in busy transit along the M2 motorway which hugged the shoreline of Belfast Lough below – as akin to "a constant stream of insects scurrying along in unnecessary haste, all intensely obsessed with their own, and too often other people's, problems." The sight of his fellow citizens so reduced in size made him question the inflated importance they – himself included – often attached to so many mundane concerns. He felt the experience was a positive one: "Everyone should come up here once in a while – it would help them see their lives in better perspective, and might even make some of them question why they treat each other the way they do."

I must admit that on my own frequent walks to the summit my thoughts are far less philosophical, and the only feeling the sight of the motorway traffic below evokes for me is intense relief that I am well away from its noise and smell. Nevertheless, I do have occasion to use the summit for a purpose which would certainly have met my departed friend's approval.

Although my community involvement is primarily concerned with promoting social change, it is frequently supplemented by another interest – that of stimulating awareness of the shared heritage of the Ulster people. The community groups I work with often request that I take young people on excursions to antiquities around the periphery of Belfast, and sometimes further afield. I find there is no better way to start such an excursion than with a walk - weather permitting – to the summit of the Cave Hill, or at least to the excellen viewpoint sited just below the caves.

From such a vantage point past history can be made to feel more tangible, les distant. It is an appropriate place to point out a myriad of facts about thes young people's shared heritage:

- The ancient earthen ditch which cuts off what is now known as 'MacArts' Fort' allows me to talk about the early habitation of this island, in the hop that the knowledge that Ireland has been inhabited since 6500 BC might pu our present obsession with '1690' and '1916' into a more realistic and les divisive perspective.

- I point across Belfast Lough to locate Bangor, then inform the young peopl that the monastic settlement which was founded there in 555 AD by S Comgall held a pre-eminent place in European history, for it was from ther that men such as Columbanus departed on their great missionary journey to barbarian Europe, and in so doing laid the foundations for the revival o European civilisation and culture.

- I follow this up by explaining that it was also this part of our island which i accepted as being the cradle of written Irish literature, and one of the products of that creativity – the *Táin*, or 'Cattle Raid of Cooley' – is the *oldes* story, written in a vernacular language, in western European literature.

- If the curiosity of the young people has been whetted sufficiently I furthe point out that during the American War of Independence young America won its first naval battle when John Paul Jones, the 'Father of the American Navy', sailed up Belfast Lough and captured the British warship *HMS Drak* in 1778. Almost a quarter of a million Ulster men and women had already emigrated to America by then, and many of these 'Scots-Irish' formed the backbone of the American revolutionary armies.

- I also explain that the summit was the place where Wolfe Tone and the Belfast Presbyterians leaders of the United Irishmen swore an oath to fight for the independence of Ireland, and I ask my young audience to reflect on the present-day reality of that legacy: the young Catholics to ask themselves whether they believe present-day Republicanism would still be recognisable to those 18th century radicals; the young Protestants to ask themselves whether they feel *their* community has lost much by dissociating itself from that idealistic period in their history when the popular toast was: 'May the Northern lights ever illuminate the Irish nation.'

- The ability to see the whole of Belfast laid out below us also helps me to explain how clusters of population grew up around the various industries, and how the present 'religious geography' of Belfast emerged among and between those clusters of working-class people.

Then, finally, if the visibility is good, I point to the outline of land lying on the horizon, before turning to the young people to ask them to tell me what it is. Although a minority of the young people can often do this, I am regularly surprised by the uncertainty expressed by the majority. "The County Antrim coast" or "The Ards Peninsula" are their most frequent responses, or more usually a shrug of the shoulders. "It's Scotland," I tell them, then watch their expressions. Surprise... disbelief... Finally, acceptance... "I didn't realise it was that close." The fact that they can even identify buildings by using binoculars only increases their surprise.

I feel that by seeing for themselves that Ireland and Scotland are, quite literally, only a short boat journey apart, it must become more difficult to adhere to the widespread belief (held by members of *both* communities) that the Scottish Presbyterians who arrived in Ulster for the 17th century Plantation were an almost alien race whose ancestors had no contact with Ireland prior to that. Even many of those who acknowledge contact between the two countries, still manage to 'colour' it quite selectively. One young Catholic spoke to me with obvious pride of Irish links with Scotland's Gaelic Highlanders, but couldn't see a similar link between these Catholic Highlanders and Presbyterian Lowlanders. Similarly, a young Shankill Road Protestant assured me that the people who support Glasgow Rangers football team are "totally different" from those who support Glasgow Celtic. If the two sets of supporters, I asked him, ever got round to supporting *one* team, and all embraced *one* religion, would they then be the same people? He gave my question earnest thought, then shook his head negatively: "They couldn't be, they're quite different."

Belfast's Cave Hill

Such responses seemed to indicate that the 'ethnic' division (which is popularly assumed to exist alongside the religious division) between the people of Ulster had been transferred, through 'guilt by association', to the people of Scotland. "If the communities in Ulster represent two separate peoples", the reasoning seemed to go, "then the people of Scotland to whom *my* community is related, must be different to the people of Scotland to whom *their* community is related."

Such highly selective communal attitudes, apart from revealing the failure of our education system to foster a more accurate awareness of our real history and heritage, will have to be challenged and overcome if there is to be any hope of a true peace between the communities in Northern Ireland. I don't believe such a task is insurmountable. On the contrary, when I stand atop Belfast's Cave Hill I often feel that not only is Scotland tantalisingly close – in the physical sense – but the possibility of engendering a new appreciation of the rich and varied, but nevertheless *shared*, culture belonging to all our young people, is tantalisingly close also.

This pamphlet is aimed at furthering such a possibility. It is not an exhaustive list of all Ulster's Scottish 'connections', but a selection of significant episodes which have proven to me at least that the peoples of Ireland and Scotland – and thereby many of the people of Ulster, who are an obvious amalgamation of the two – are not the two completely alien races of people so often depicted in popular imagery, but two peoples who share an ancient kinship, and have continued to interrelate with each other throughout their history. The two communities in Northern Ireland at present might imagine they have little in common, and continue to perpetrate terrible deeds against one another as if to emphasise their differences, but sooner or later they will have to come to terms with the *shared* nature of their historical and cultural heritage. Perhaps that knowledge might assist them to sit down together and find less painful ways of resolving their real and imagined divisions, rather than the present unnecessary violence, with all its tragic individual and communal consequences.

[In exploring the links between Ulster and Scotland I am obviously not unaware that the make-up of the Ulster people owes much to many more countries than just Scotland – indeed, new immigrants from around the world continue to make their own contribution even today. However, the background to Ulster's present communal divide is primarily attributed to the irreconcilable divisions supposed to have existed between Scottish 'Planter' and Irish 'Gael', and so it is to address this aspect of our history that this pamphlet is concerned.]

Ulster's Scottish Connection

Rebuilding the Bridge

The geographical features of a country are often used to 'prove' the veracity of its political boundaries. Dr Patrick Hillery, Irish Minister for External Affairs, in a speech to the United Nations Security Council in 1969, spoke of the Irish nation as being an "entity which nature and history have made one".[1] However, the conferring by 'nature' of an island status in other parts of the world has not necessarily gone hand-in-hand with the political unity which Dr Hillery claimed "is so self-evident as not to require argument" for Ireland.

Indeed, others *could* engage him in such an argument, ironically using the same discipline of geography to reinforce their point. A Northern Irish Protestant, jealously protective of the 'Union' with mainland Britain, could easily find 'support' in the following words from geographer Estyn Evans:

> It is in the north-east that Ireland's connections with Britain are oldest, closest and most enduring; and if we turn to geological history, whether to the remote pre-Cambrian and Primary or to the Tertiary and Quaternary periods, it is in Ulster that the physical relations between the two islands can be most clearly discerned.[2]

Ask an old country storyteller if he believes Ulster has a 'link' with Scotland and he might reply, with a mischievous glint in his eye: "sure now, didn't the Irish giant Finn MacCool once build a bridge over to there." Legend has made much of the fact that the unique hexagonal-shaped basalt columns of the Giant's Causeway, the Antrim coast's world-famous geological wonder, are also found 75 miles away in seaswept caves on the island of Staffa, off the western coast of Scotland.

One version of the legend has it that Finn MacCool was so intent on doing battle with an adversary, the Scottish giant Finn Gall, he constructed a causeway across the North Channel, driving the columns into place one by one. However, the task completed, he prudently returned to Ireland to rest and replenish his energy before the coming encounter.

Meanwhile, curious as to what this unknown rival was up to, Finn Gall crossed the causeway to Ulster, only to come upon his Irish counterpart asleep on the grass. Just then Finn MacCool's wife appeared; relying on her quick Ulster wit and shrewdness she told the visitor not to dare waken her sleeping 'child' or her husband would be none too pleased when he came along. Alarmed at what size the father might be if the offspring was already this large, Finn Gall fled back to Scotland, destroying the causeway after him as he went. So to this day only the extremities remain, pounded and battered by the forces of the sea.

Whatever the form of the 'natural' evidence, or the source of the legends, my purpose here is neither to reinforce nor undermine the case for Irish unity or conversely the Union with Britain, but to undo the damage done by Finn Gall and help rebuild the bridge between the peoples on either side of the North Channel. And although a foreign tourist might see the beauty of the natural setting as the most obvious link between Scotland and Ireland – with their equal share of spectacular mountains, dramatic sea-cliffs, sylvan valleys and tranquil hamlets – my primary concern is with the "two great and intimately associated peoples" of Scotland and Ireland – as W C Mackenzie once described them.[3] So it is to the earliest evidence of contact between these two peoples that I now turn.

The Giant's Causeway —
Legendary 'link' with Scotland

In the Beginning

The archaeological evidence suggests that the first settlers in Ireland arrived around 6500 BC in the period known as the Mesolithic or Middle Stone Age, probably coming from the Galloway region of Scotland or Cumbria in northern England.[4]

In the Neolithic period which followed, numerous stone burial monuments were erected. One particular type, the *court cairns*, as well as being distributed around the northern half of Ireland, are also found in south-west Scotland, a fact which led Séan O Ríordáin to comment: "The tombs and the finds from

8

them form a continuous province joined rather than divided by the narrow waters of the North Channel."[5] Some archaeologists have labelled these tombs the 'Clyde-Carlingford cairns' to signify the close connection between the two regions.

Later, during the Bronze Age, a particular type of pot, known as a 'beaker', made its appearance in Europe. Because of the widespread distribution of these beakers it was once assumed there was a movement across Europe of a Beaker people, but current thinking is more in favour of viewing it simply as the movement of a new commodity. Nevertheless, as J P Mallory and T E McNeill point out:

> ...the concentration of beaker finds in Ulster, especially along the north coast, suggests that they entered Ulster from Scotland. We cannot be certain about whether 'they' means a new people or a just a new pot but the existence of substantial Beaker settlements in the Western Isles of Scotland does suggest the possibility that there was some movement of people.[6]

Such population movements across the North Channel would hardly be surprising. With north-east Ireland and south-west Scotland separated by only thirteen miles at their closest points, the waterway between Scotland and Ireland would not have been seen as a barrier, as we tend to view it today, but as an important route of commerce and communication.

Present thinking among historians and archaeologists is increasingly coming to accept the importance of these ancient pre-Celtic inhabitants of Ireland and Scotland as our predominant ancestors. Archaeologist Peter Woodman has pointed out:

> The gene pool of the Irish was probably set by the end of the Stone Age when there were very substantial numbers of people present and the landscape had already been frequently altered. The Irish are essentially Pre-Indo-European, they are not physically Celtic. No invasion since could have been sufficiently large to alter this fact completely.[7]

Further, the relationship *between* the people of the two islands is also felt to relate to that distant past. As Liam de Paor commented:

> The gene pool of the Irish... is probably very closely related to the gene pools of highland Britain... Within that fringe area, relationships, both cultural and genetic, almost certainly go back to a much more distant time than that uncertain period when Celtic languages and customs came to dominate both Great Britain and Ireland. Therefore, so far as the physical make-up of the Irish goes... they share these origins with their fellows in the neighbouring parts – the north and west – of the next-door island of Great Britain.[8]

So, right from the beginning of our history, Ulster's 'connection' with Scotland was already well established.

'Isles of the Pretani'

What did the Irish themselves say about any such kinship with the people of Scotland, once the age of writing had dawned?

Some time between 330 and 300 BC the Greek geographer Pytheas, in his *Concerning the Ocean*, called the British Isles the 'Isles of the Pretani'. This is the first recorded name given to the inhabitants of our two islands. But did these inhabitants consider themselves to be related in any way? Ian Adamson has summarised various ancient references which seem to indicate that some of those in Scotland and Ireland certainly did:

> [In the later Irish literature] 'Pretani' became 'Cruthin' and when medieval Irish writers referred to these people it is clear they considered them to inhabit both Ireland and Scotland. One writer stated that 'thirty kings of the Cruthin ruled Ireland and Scotland from Ollam to Fiachna mac Baetáin,' and that 'seven kings of the Cruthin of Scotland ruled Ireland in Tara' – thereby identifying, as T F O'Rahilly notes, "the Cruthin of Ireland with those of Scotland". Others refer to Scotland as the 'land of the Cruthin', while in a poem written in the eleventh or twelfth century the author tells us that the *Cruthnig* made up a section of the population of Scotland. The Annals of Tigernach, The Pictish Chronicle, St Berchan, the Albanic Duan, the Book of Deer and John of Fordun plainly show that the name Cruthin was applied to the inhabitants of both Scotland and Ireland. [9]

These ancient 'Pretanic' people have given rise to much debate, indeed controversy, among academics. Were they pre-Celtic? Some believe they were: Francis Byrne speaks of the Cruthin of north-east Ireland as being part of the earlier peoples who "survived under the Celtic overlordship" [10]; Charles Doherty treads more warily, saying that their "distant ancestors... may even have been pre-Celtic." [11] The Pretanic people of Scotland were to become known as 'Picts', and the little that is known about their language clearly identifies them as pre-Celtic. [12]

Whatever the possible link between the Cruthin of east Ulster and the Picts of Scotland it is believed that each group were in the majority in their respective areas. Francis Byrne says the Cruthin formed "the majority of the population" of Ulster [13], while Liam de Paor points out: "The Picts undoubtedly contributed much to the make-up of the medieval kingdom of Scotland, forming probably the bulk of its population." [14]

However, whether these two population groups did share a close kinship cannot as yet be proven by the available archaeological evidence, though neither too has the claim of the ancient Irish writers that "the Cruthin of both countries formed one people in remote times." [15] been disproved.

Dalriada

Although it is now widely accepted that when the Celts came to Ireland they only represented a minority of the population, some of their powerful dynasties eventually became ascendant in many parts of the island – in particular the Uí Néill, who made strong inroads into the territory traditionally attributed to ancient Ulster. Following the destruction around 450 AD of the Ulster capital at Emain Macha (now Navan Fort) 'Ulster' as a territorial entity was confined to territory east of the River Bann. A massive earthwork wall was erected to delimit part of the new reduced boundary, and the Ulstermen struggled to retain a degree of independence for the next 700 years.

Possibly because of the pressure of these Uí Néill territorial gains and the subsequent contraction of Ulster, groups within the Northern population began to move across the North Channel, in particular the Dál Riata, who settled Argyll and the islands along the western coast of Scotland. The Venerable Bede, writing in the 8th century, states that this land was obtained from the local Pictish people "either by fair means or force". The kings of the Dál Riata soon claimed sovereignty over territory on both sides of the North Channel, and Fergus MacErc forsook his Irish capital of Dunseverick around 500 to established his main residence in Argyll.

The Romans had known these Irish raiders as the 'Scotti', Ireland itself becoming known as 'Scotia'. These 'Scotti' founded a rival 'Scottish' kingdom to the Picts. Eventually, in the ninth century, the Scottish king Kenneth MacAlpine, through both conquest and royal intermarriage, became king of both Scots and Picts, and his successors greatly extended the territory which from now on was to become known as 'Scotland'. These settlers had absorbed the Gaelic language while in Ulster, and they carried it with them to their new homeland. This new language, over the succeeding centuries, was to spread throughout Scotland, further cementing the link between the two countries.

The Early Christian Era

The history of Christianity in Scotland effectively starts in 397 AD with the settlement established by St Ninian at Candida Casa (now Whithorn) in Galloway. His settlement, based on the system developed by St Martin of Tours, whom Ninian is thought to have visited, was quite unlike other religious communities in Britain, and was to become the model for countless more.

> He settled his monks in an arrangement of cells which enabled them to live in solitary reflection while at the same time sharing in a corporate life. In honour of his own teacher, he dedicated the first stone church to be built in Britain to Martin; and he called it Candida Casa as a reminder of the white hut which St Hilary gave to St Martin at Poitiers. [16]

Ninian's fame grew with the church, and the extent of his work and that of other monks from Candida Casa is readily apparent from the widespread incidence of Ninian dedications that are found all over Scotland, from Shetland in the north down to Stirling, and from Bute in the west to Aberdeen in the east. The proximity of Galloway to Ulster also meant that evangelism was easily carried across the North Channel. Finnian, a student at Candida Casa, founded his own community at Moville on Strangford Lough in County Down, and one tradition even has it that Portpatrick on the Rhinns of Galloway was the place from where St Patrick journeyed to Ireland.

This religious influence was not restricted to one direction only, for that great religious figure of Ireland, St Columba (Columb-Cille), was to prove of equal importance in the evangelisation of Scotland. Columba studied under St Finnian at Movilla, where he was ordained deacon, and, according to the *Annals of Ulster*, founded Derry in 545.

The ruins known as Ninian's Chapel

Ninian's Cave

"The spirit of Ninian is more easily felt in the sea cave in the cliffs that overhang the rocky beach of Glasserton to the west of the Machars promontory. In common with his teacher Martin, and in the tradition of the Desert Fathers, Ninian sought regular solitary retreats. It was to this cave that he came. It is a wild and lonely place even today, and even in summer, for all that it is so close to farms and villages. Long after the saint's death the place was used by men who wanted to withdraw from the world for a while. The crosses they cut into its walls take their chance with the weather; but those on the stones which were found about its entrance at the end of the last century are now preserved in the priory museum." [16]

Columba was a prince of the Northern Uí Néill, and no stranger to the political intrigues of the period. Indeed, the legend surrounding him tells us that his reason for leaving Ireland was the result of a squabble which he partly instigated, and which he in anger tried to resolve on the battlefield.

Many of those in the service of the church occupied themselves with the transcribing of manuscripts, a painstaking task which necessitated great patience and dedication. Now Columba had made a copy of a psalter belonging to Finnian. However, Finnian insisted that he had no right to do so and claimed that as the copy had been made without his permission it therefore belonged to him, not to Columba. The two men took their dispute to the high king, Diarmait, Columba's case being that he had made the copy for the public good, no harm had been done to the original, and therefore he was entitled to retain his copy. To Columba's annoyance the high king, in possibly the first statement of copyright law, concluded: "To every cow its calf and to every book its copy."

Furious, Columba gathered his kinsmen together to do battle on his behalf. The ensuring clash, at the battle of Cúl Dreimhne, resulted in much slaughter, and Columba, appalled at what he had instigated, resolved as a penance to go into voluntary exile. He departed Ulster and journeyed to the small island of Iona, close to the coast of Argyll.

However, leaving aside the legend, there may have been other factors which led Columba to travel to Iona. Iona had long been a holy place before Columba arrived, not only for Christians but also for the Druids. One possibility is that this area of Argyll, long peopled by Columba's own countrymen, the Scots of Dalriada, had begun to lapse from the church, and "the real reason for his leaving Ireland in the first place could well have been to undertake a missionary journey to recall people to the true faith." [16]

Whatever the truth of the matter, the community Columba founded on Iona was to prove of immense importance to the religious and the cultural history of Scotland. The *Encyclopedia Britannica* in 1886 lauded his achievements thus:

> He frequently revisited Ireland and took part in its wars: the militant spirit is strongly marked in his character; but most of his time was devoted to the administration of his monastery of Iona, and to the planting of other churches and religious houses in the neighbouring isles and mainland, till his death in 597. None of the remains now found in almost every island – not even those in Iona itself – date from his time, when wood was still used for building. But the original foundations of the churches of Skye and Tiree were his work; those extending from Bute and Cantyre – on Islay, Oronsay, Colonsay, Mull, Eigg, Lewis, Harris, Benbecula, and even the distant St Kilda – to Loch Arkaig on the northern mainland of Scottish Dalriada are to be ascribed to him or his immediate followers or successors in the abbacy, as well as those in the country of the Picts, from the Orkneys to Deer in Buchan. The churches which received his name farther south were later foundations in his honour. [17]

And so it was that not only with regard to the political unification of the country, but also in the establishment of its church, people from Ulster played a vital role in the early history of Scotland.

Ruins on the island of Iona

North Channel Culture Province

The energy of the early church was not only directed to religious and even political pursuits, but to cultural matters as well.

Long before the arrival of Christianity, and the subsequent development of writing, Irish society had attached great importance to oral tradition, and those with responsibility for maintaining this tradition were held in high regard.

> The laws, the genealogies of the clans, the history of the tribes, were all composed and recited in verse. Consequently, the most important persons in the land, next to the chiefs, were the Fílés. It was their business to act as law-givers, arbitrators, genealogists, and historians, besides being the story-tellers and poets of the tribe. They were treated with the greatest respect, and were constantly in attendance on the chief, taking part in his councils.[18]

With the advent of Christianity and its practice of manuscript writing in the *scriptoria* of the monasteries, the clergy, as well as their obvious preoccupation with religious books, also began to commit the laws, customs and history of their countrymen to writing. Such diversity no doubt also served to enhance the Church's reputation, for pagan learned men, poets and jurists still survived alongside them as an important element in society. As Francis Byrne pointed out: "Irish monasticism cultivated learning and so ensured respect in a society where scholarship was held in high regard." [13]

Proinsias Mac Cana believed that it was in the monastic settlements centred around Bangor in County Down (where St Comgall had established his monastery in 555) that the activities of the monastic *literati* "assumed something of the impetus and cohesiveness of a cultural movement", so much so that "one may with due reservations speak of this region of south-east Ulster as the cradle of written Irish literature." [19] Mac Cana felt that one of the primary reasons for such creativity was the cross-fertilisation between this region and nearby Scotland:

> Isolation tends towards stagnation, or at least a circumscribed vision, while conversely intercourse and cultural commerce encourage a greater intellectual curiosity and awareness, a greater readiness to adapt old ways and experiment with new ones. For such intercourse the east-Ulster region was ideally situated. It was a normal landing-place for travellers from northern Britain, which during the sixth and seventh centuries probably presented a more dramatic clash and confluence of cultures than any other part of Britain or Ireland; and, in addition, the religious, social and political ties that linked north-eastern Ireland and north-western Britain – particularly in that period – were numerous and close. Archaeologists speak of an 'Irish Sea culture-province' with its western flank in Ireland and its eastern flank in Britain; one might with comparable justification speak of a North Channel culture-province within which obtained a free currency of ideas, literary, intellectual and artistic. [19]

The Ulster Tales ... Cúchulainn trains in Alba

Among the products of this flowering of literary creativeness was a group of tales known collectively as the Ulster Cycle, traditionally felt to depict the North of Ireland in the first centuries AD. While these stories give us a glimpse, albeit highly romanticised, into Ireland's Iron Age – its 'Heroic' Age – of more importance is the prominent position they hold in this island's cultural heritage.

In the tales the main characters frequently move between Ulster and Scotland. Cúchulainn, perhaps the greatest of Ireland's legendary heroes – and after whom, according to legend, the Cuillin mountains of Skye are named – travelled to Alba (Scotland) to receive specialist training in the fighting arts from a renowned female warrior, Scáthach. When Cúchulainn eventually reached Scáthach's abode, he found it encircled by a deep ravine, with the only access provided by a bridge. But this was no ordinary bridge, its 'magic' qualities being designed to prevent an easy traverse:

> Wonderful was the sight that bridge afforded when anyone would leap upon it, for it narrowed until it became as narrow as the hair of one's head, and the second time it shortened until it became as short as an inch, and the third time it grew slippery until it was as slippery as an eel of the river, and the fourth time it rose up on high against you until it was as tall as the mast of a ship.[20]

Some of Scáthach's pupils who were gathered nearby informed Cúchulainn it would be impossible for him to cross the bridge until he underwent lengthy training, but the Ulster warrior was in no mood for any such delay. Three times he attempted to cross but was violently flung back. Then, so enraged that he went into his warrior-spasm – with which he was frequently afflicted – he leapt across the ravine so quickly the bridge had no time to fly up past him. This feat so impressed Scáthach she accepted Cúchulainn as her special pupil and the training he received at her hands was put to good effect when he was later called upon to defend Ulster from an invasion by Queen Maeve and the 'Men of Ireland'.

. . . Deirdre of the Sorrows

One of the finest, and deservedly best-loved, of the stories of the Ulster Cycle is the 'Fate of the Children of Usnach'. In the story king Conor MacNessa of Ulster and his warriors were feasting at the home of Conor's chief story-teller when their host's wife gave birth to a daughter. Conor called upon his Druid to prophesy the child's future. To everyone's concern the prophesy claimed that the girl would grow up to be exceedingly beautiful but her beauty would be the cause of a terrible catastrophe to befall Ulster. Horrified, the warriors demanded that the child be slain, but Conor prevented this, saying the girl would be reared in isolation and then married to him when she came of age. In this way, he argued, her beauty could not be the cause of dangerous jealousy.

*"A woman with twisted yellow tresses, green-irised eyes of great beauty and cheeks flushed like the foxglove...
I say that whiter than the snow is the white treasure of her teeth;
Parthian-red, her lip's lustre.
Ulster's chariot-warriors will deal many a blow for her."* [21]

17

And so Deirdre grew to womanhood in a special enclosure close to the king's palace at Emain Macha, until a sequence of events led her to meet Naisi, one of the three sons of Usnach. The two young people fell madly in love, though Naisi was naturally fearful of Conor's wrath should he ever find out about the relationship. Nevertheless, love proved stronger than prudence and the lovers finally eloped under cover of darkness. Conor was furious, ordering that the pair be hunted down, and they were forced to move from place to place.

Finally, accompanied by Naisi's brothers, they sought sanctuary in Scotland, and in the lovely Glen Etive at last managed to live a more normal life. Unfortunately, Conor discovered their whereabouts and enticed them to return to Ulster with the promise that all was forgiven. Deirdre remained disbelieving of Conor's change of heart, but more poignantly, in her farewell lament, she revealed how much she had taken her adopted homeland to her heart:

Delightful land, yon eastern land, Alba, with its wonders;
I would not have come hither out of it had I not come with Naisi.

The Vale of Láidh, oh in the Vale of Láidh I used to sleep under soft coverlet;
fish and venison and the fat of the badger were my repast in the Vale of Láidh.

The Vale of Masan, oh the vale of Masan, high its harts-tongue, fair its stalks;
we used to enjoy a rocking sleep above the grassy verge of Masan.

The Vale of Etive, oh, the Vale of Etive! In it I raised my first house;
lovely was its wood (when seen) on rising; the milking-house of the sun was the Vale of Etive.

Glen Darua, oh Glen Darua! My love to every one who enjoys it;
sweet the voice of the cuckoo upon bending bough upon the cliff above Glen Darua.

Dear is Droighin over the strong shore. Dear are its waters over pure sand;
I would never have come from it had I not come with my love.

On their return to Ulster Deirdre's feelings of foreboding intensified:

O Naisi, view the cloud
That I see here on the sky,
I see over Emania green
A chilling cloud of blood-tinged red.

Tragically, her suspicions were to be confirmed. Conor ordered the three sons of Usnach captured and beheaded, but this act of gross treachery so outraged many of Ulster's warriors they fell upon Emain Macha, inflicting great carnage upon Conor's household, before departing into exile.

Deirdre, refusing to accept the advances of Conor and in constant grief for her dead lover, finally leapt to her death from the king's chariot.

Galloway

The movement of people from Ulster to Argyll and the establishment of Dalriada has tended to overshadow a later movement across the North Channel – that of a migration to Galloway. As Charles Thomas wrote:

> An admirable guide to the early Irish settlement could be constructed from the distribution of certain place-name elements – particularly those relating to simple natural features. [Such names are found in] an intense localized concentration in the double peninsula of the Rhinns of Galloway, opposite Antrim. No special historical sources describe what now looks like another early Irish colony here – possibly of the sixth century. But isolated archaeological finds from Galloway, the spread of a type of early ecclesiastical site (the enclosed developed cemetery) which may be regarded as Irish-inspired, and several minor pointers in the same direction, are mounting to reliable evidence for a separate settlement in this south-western area." [22]

We have already touched upon the religious 'connection' between the two areas. The church at Bangor would have had strong links with this region, indeed a Bangor monk became Abbot of St Ninian's old monastery of Candida Casa at the end of the sixth century, and churches in Galloway were often dedicated to saints popular in Ulster.

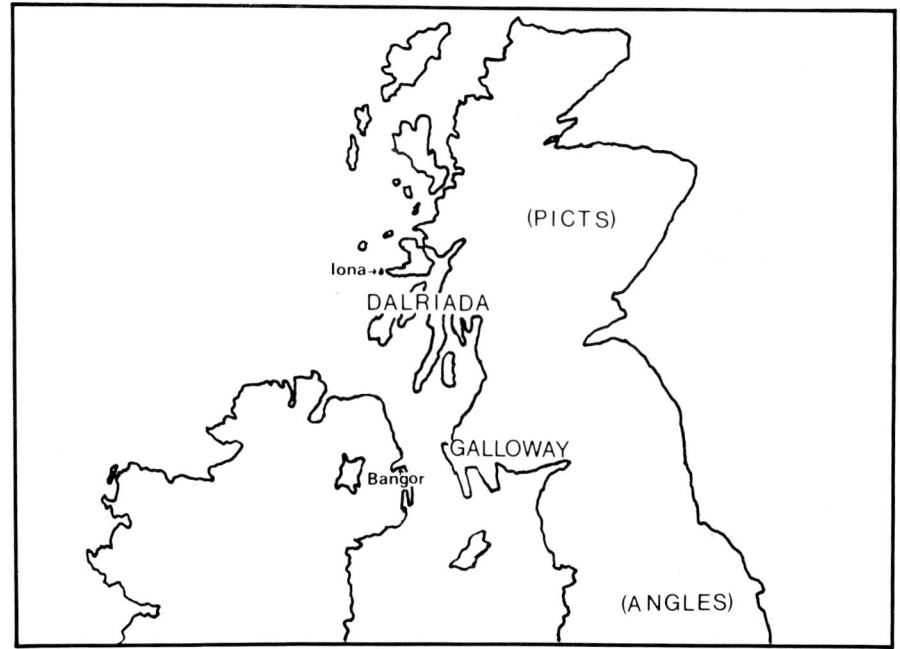

A Scot becomes King of Ireland

Robert the Bruce in hiding

On 24 June 1314 the Scots, under Robert the Bruce, defeated the English at the battle of Bannockburn. For Robert Bruce it was the culmination of a long personal struggle, which had necessitated a period of hiding on Rathlin Island, off the Antrim coast. One of our most popular legends relates that while sheltering in a cave there, and filled with despair, he was taught a lesson in perseverance from a spider trying to build its web, and realised that: 'if at first you don't succeed, try and try again.'

Following this victory for Scottish independence O'Neill of Tyrone offered to make Robert's brother Edward King of Ireland, and in May 1315 Edward Bruce landed at Larne. He was joined by Robert Bissett with the Scots of Antrim and by Donald O'Neill son of Brian of Tyrone.

To oppose him stood Richard, the Red Earl of Ulster, in alliance with Felim O'Connor and the army of Connacht. The adversaries eventually faced each other across the waters of the Bann. At this point O'Connor deserted the Red Earl who had to retreat and was subsequently defeated in battle near Ballymena. Edward was crowned King of Ireland on 1 May, 1316, in the presence of a large assembly of Irish and Scottish nobles. However, his death in battle near Dundalk in 1318 finally brought the Scottish invasion to an end.

Edward Bruce had brought with him some 6,000 Scottish mercenaries – the 'galloglass' – and over the next few centuries the importation by the Irish of a constant stream of these Scots (many of whom were to be rewarded with land by the Gaelic chiefs) was to have an important effect on Irish warfare. As Edmund Curtis pointed out:

> In the military and political history of Ireland the galloglass proved a turning point. Up to this the Irish, though brave enough, in their light dress were no match for the heavily armed Normans, but now they found in these Scottish mercenaries trained and traditional soldiers who could endure the Norman arrows and repulse their foot, and who before long turned the tide of battle against them. To them we may attribute much of the resurgence of Gaelic Ireland in the next three centuries. [23]

The Plantation

It was Ulster's Gaelic chieftains who had always put up the most determined resistance to the English, and effective Crown jurisdiction in Ireland gradually became confined to an ever-shrinking area around Dublin, termed 'the Pale'. During the reign of Elizabeth I, however, the English were to pursue their attempts at conquest with much more determination.

The response of the Northern chiefs was a rebellion which shook English government in Ireland to its foundations. In 1594 Hugh O'Donnell defeated an English army at the 'Ford of the Biscuits', and the following year, with Hugh O'Neill joining the rebellion, the English sustained heavy losses at Clontibret. Worse was to follow for the English when they were dramatically defeated at the Yellow Ford, to the south of Lough Neagh, in 1598, a defeat which inspired uprisings throughout Ireland.

However, the English recovered and once again resistance in all but Ulster was crushed. Then, in 1601, a Spanish force, coming to aid the Ulster chieftains, landed at Kinsale in the far south of Ireland. O'Neill preferred fighting in his own territory of Ulster, but expertly avoiding English forces sent to intercept him, he and his army marched south. At the ensuing battle the English defeated the Irish forces and finally broke the rebellion. O'Neill returned to Ulster but eventually submitted to Mountjoy in 1603.

Four years later, on 4 September 1607, after continued harassment by Crown officials, Hugh O'Neill, Rory O'Donnell, and the flower of many Ulster families, abandoned their people and sailed from Rathmullan into voluntary exile in Europe. Following this 'Flight of the Earls', their estates, around 750,000 acres, were confiscated by the English government.

Donegal Castle, built by the O'Donnells in 1474, was the residence of Hugh Roe O'Donnell, last chief of Tir Connell. Extensive renovations were carried out in the 17th century.

The English now decided to plant settlers in the confiscated lands, partly with the intention that it might be a way of 'civilising' this most rebellious part of Ireland once and for all.

It was Sir Arthur Chichester who, in 1610, was to be "the chief architect of the Plantation in Ulster". [24] Yet, he was annoyed that while good English settlers were being sent to the territories now opening up in the new land of America, most of those being sent to Ulster were Scots. Chichester, who had no real love for the Irish, was no more enamoured by the Scots.

> He had no special affection for Scotsmen, high or low, gentle or simple, and besides he had spent much of his time and ingenuity ever since his coming to Ireland, in the work of repelling and expelling Islesmen and other Northern Scots from the coasts of Ulster. [25]

If Chichester had been fully aware of the frequent movements of people across the North Channel throughout history, he might have realised the impossibility of such a task. As P L Henry pointed out:

> The mould was fixed in ancient times and modern developments continue ancient associations. We need but think of the Pictish Kingdoms in both areas, of the Ulster-Scottish Kingdom of Dalriada from the last quarter of the 5th to the close of the 8th century, of the Scottish Kingdom founded under Gaelic leadership in 842, of Irish relations with the Kingdom of the Hebrides and Argyll from the 12th century, particularly the immigration of Hebridean soldiers (galloglass) from the 13th to the 16th century. There was a constant coming and going between North East Ireland and Western Scotland. The Glens of Antrim were in the hands of Scottish MacDonalds by 1400, and for the next two hundred years Gaelic-speaking Scots came in large numbers. The 17th century immigration of a numerous Scots element need not be considered outside the preceding series. [26]

Because of these ancient associations many of the Lowland Scots settlers may indeed be considered as returning to the home of their ancestors – F J Bigger wrote that "When the Galloway planters came to Ulster they were only returning to their own lands like emigrants returning home again." [27] However, they were to be different from the local population in one very important respect – most of the newcomers were Protestants. And it has been the religious difference between these Scottish 'Planters' and the native Irish that has – throughout the succeeding centuries – successfully obscured all the other elements of their history, heritage, and even ancestry, which the two groups of people once shared. Even in language the 'newcomers' retained an affinity to the Irish among whom they were now being planted. As Ian Adamson pointed out:

> Firstly there was a significant group who spoke Gaelic and it seems that Scottish Gaelic speakers were intelligible to the Irish at this period. (Indeed, the first book ever to be printed in Irish Gaelic was a translation of the Calvinist *Book of Common Order*, commonly called John Knox's Liturgy, published in Edinburgh in 1567 for the use of Presbyterians.) Secondly,

the language of the others was not the standard English of today but Lallans, which is derived from the Central Scots language, known in Scotland as 'Inglis'. This Lallans language is still spoken in the north-east of Ulster and in Donegal, where contact with Scotland through settlement and commerce has been close. The Scottish speech is in some ways an older form of the English language grouping than standard English. Church and state have been just as antagonistic to Lallans as they have been to Gaelic itself, leading to as great a contraction of the Scots-speaking districts as the Gaelic-speaking districts of Ulster. [9]

Although the plantation never proved to be the radical transformation the Crown had intended, the Catholic Irish had sufficient reason to nurture a seething resentment, and this finally exploded into rebellion in 1641.

At the beginning of the uprising the rebels stated that the Scottish Presbyterians should not be harmed because of their 'Gaelic' origins. A report presented to the House of Commons in June, 1642, said: "In the infancy of the Rebellion the rebels made open proclamations, upon pain of death, that no Scotchman should be stirred in body, goods or lands, and that they should to this purpose write over the lyntels of their doors that they were Scotchmen, and so destruction might pass over their families." Furthermore the report's author related that he had read a letter, "sent by two of the rebels, Colonel Nugent and Colonel O'Gallagher... which was directed to, 'Our honourable friends, the gentlemen of the never conquered Scotch nation'."

However, although the English settlers suffered most, any distinction between them soon vanished, with Scottish Presbyterians being butchered and Protestants retaliating in kind. Sectarian violence was now to become an ever-present feature of Irish history.

Rebellion!

23

The rebels were disunited in their tactics and objectives, and Irish resistance was already faltering when Oliver Cromwell landed in Dublin in August 1649, with the intention of restoring this "Bleeding Nation of Ireland to its former happiness and tranquillity". The ruthless way he carried out this intention left a further legacy of bitterness on the part of Irish Catholics towards England. The rebellion ensured that the religious difference was to become of paramount importance in Irish politics. Even the Battle of the Boyne in 1690, which was only a small part of a European power struggle against Louis XIV of France, became, for Ireland, a great symbolic clash between the two religions, and William's victory over his father-in-law James II was hailed, or lamented, as a triumph of Protestantism over Catholicism, and of 'Planter' over 'Gael'.

The Plantation and its aftermath is now etched deeply into the folk memory of the two communities in Ulster. Yet, no matter how differently they view that period, there is one point of agreement – both 'sides' somehow believe that they have remained completely separate and distinct communities ever since. Yet Ireland, notwithstanding its deep divisions, could not have remained immune from one of the normal evolutionary trends of human history – the intermingling of peoples. Contrary to popular belief the 'Planters' did not drive the 'Gaels' off the planted territories en masse; while the Gaelic landlords were certainly dispossessed, it is now realised that the entire pre-plantation population was not. As historian A T Q Stewart points out:

> Neither the undertakers nor the London companies found it expedient or possible to clear all the native Irish from their lands, and therefore they accepted them as tennants, violating their contracts with the Crown in order to do so. Without the Irish tenants it is doubtful whether the Scots and English planters could have made such limited progress as they had by 1641. The great concealed factor in this whole 'British' plantation is the part played by the relatively undisturbed Irish population in building the towns, fortified bawns and planter castles, and in developing the resources of forests, rivers and loughs... When we remember that the servitors and Irish grantees were actually permitted to take Irish tenants, it becomes clear beyond doubt that a very substantial proportion of the original population was not disturbed at all. Modern historical research on the plantation has thrown much light on this continuity of population.[28]

And if the two communities did live in such close proximity, another natural process would inevitably have occurred, one that is still going strong today. As Estyn Evans remarked:

> There was much more intermarriage, with or without the benefit of the clergy, than the conventional histories make allowance for. [2]

Nor did the religious 'divide' remain absolute. There is abundant evidence that many planters became Catholics and many native Irish became Protestants. As Ian Adamson pointed out:

The fact that many 'native Irish' became Protestants is well illustrated by the Hearth Money Rolls for the Presbyterian parishes of Stranorlar and Leck in Donegal for the year 1665, as well as by the presence of such old Cruthinic families as Rooney, Lowry, Macartan and Maguinness in the records of the Episcopalian Diocese of Dromore in South and West Down. Representatives of other well-known Gaelic families abound. Murphys, Maguires, Kellys, Lennons, Reillys, Doghertys and many others are quite numerous. In North Down, where 17th century settlement from Scotland was most successful, Brendan Adams has stated that "a large part of the native population became absorbed into the Protestant Church." Thus in a book listing subscribers to church funds in the Presbyterian church in Saintfield, Co Down, at least 20% of the names were native, pre-17th century names like Dugan, Donnan, Hanvey and Kelly. [29]

Ulick O'Connor made the same point about our current history when he wrote, of IRA hunger-striker Bobby Sands:

> It is ironic that he, who more than anyone else by his devotion to the Irish language while in Long Kesh helped to contribute to the present renaissance of the language in West Belfast, should not have a Gaelic name. (I once published a list of eleven names that could well have been those of a Protestant hockey team of boys and girls from a posh Belfast school. It was, in fact, compiled from a list of members of the Provisional IRA who had been killed in action.) You can see the influence of this mixed background in Bobby Sands' writing – Scots dialogue here and there; 'the sleekit old Brit' for instance. [30]

The people of Ulster, today more than ever before, are the unique product of this 'mixed background', and whatever changes the plantation wrought in the economic transformation of Ulster, it was as the result of the sweat and toil of *both* communities.

Doe Castle, Donegal, built by the MacSweeneys, who came from Scotland on the invitation of the O'Donnells and settled on Sheep Haven. MacSweeney na dTuath was the foster father of Red Hugh O'Donnell.

The Scots-Irish

When James II fled England to be succeeded as king by his son-in-law William of Orange, Ireland had remained strongly loyal to the Jacobite cause, and James tried to regain his throne using Ireland as a stepping-stone. But while William's 'Glorious Revolution' was taking effect in England, the Protestants of Ulster, by their defence of Derry and Enniskillen, saved Ireland for the British Crown, and when William eventually landed they were at his side for his victory at the Boyne.

Yet this loyalty to England received scant reward. The English High Church was Episcopalian and the 'Protestant Ascendancy' which now established itself in Ireland had as little regard for Presbyterianism as it had for Catholicism:

> Having reduced the rebellious Catholics by the harsh Penal Laws under William, which were based on the French Catholic legislation against Protestants, the High Church Party had gained in strength, and by the reign of Queen Anne (1702-1714) were pressing for complete conformity. In 1704 the Test act was passed which required all office holders in Ireland to take the sacrament of the Anglican Church. Although ostensibly passed to further discourage Catholicism, the real object of the Act was to place the Presbyterians on the same plane of impotence. Presbyterian

The Scots-Irish were prominent in extending the American frontier.

ministers had now no official standing and marriages performed by them were null and void. To the High Churchmen they were actually inferior to Catholic priests, who were considered lawfully ordained in the line of apostolic succession. Presbyterians and other Dissenters could not now serve in the army, the militia, the civil service, the municipal corporations, the teaching profession or the commission of the peace. At Belfast the entire Corporation was expelled, and Londonderry lost ten of its twelve aldermen (Schism Act). [9]

Severe economic pressures compounded the problem. The Woollen Act of 1699 had forbidden the export of Irish wool, making sheep rearing unprofitable, and absentee English landlords steadily increased their rents. Pushed to the limit, the Ulster Presbyterians, in 1717, began their great migration to America.

The stream of Ulster Presbyterians leaving for America became a flood, and by the time America declared for Independence, a quarter of a million Ulster men and women had emigrated there, and were estimated to have composed 15% of the population. Because of their Lowland Scots ancestry, these Ulster settlers became known in America as the 'Scotch-Irish' – although 'Scots-Irish' is nowadays the preferred spelling.

The Scots-Irish had a profound impact on their new country of domicile:

It can be said that the Scotch-Irish made three contributions to colonial

The Scots-Irish "provided some of the best fighters in the American Army. Indeed, there were those who held the Scotch-Irish responsible for the [Revolutionary] war itself." [32]

America: they settled the frontier, they founded the Kirk, and they built the school. They, more than any other group, created the first western frontier. To the Ulster Scots must largely go the credit of being the first pioneers west of the Appalachians and of opening the Mississippi Valley. [31]

Their independent streak, coupled with the hatred they had brought with them of aristocratic landlordism, had far-reaching consequences in that the Scots-Irish were to be foremost in the Revolutionary War against Britain. Indeed, the first armed clash to precede the Revolutionary War occurred in 1771 when Scots-Irish settlers fought British forces on the Alamance River in North Carolina. On 20 May 1775 they were the most prominent signatories of the Mecklenburg Declaration of Independence drawn up in Charlotte, North Carolina.

They subsequently supported the Declaration of Independence passed by the Continental Congress on 4 July 1776 and they composed the flower and backbone of Washington's army. A German captain who fought alongside the British redcoats was quite explicit: "Call this war by whatever name you may, only call it not an American rebellion; it is nothing more or less than a Scotch-Irish Presbyterian rebellion." The Pennsylvania Line, the famous force of regular troops, was of primarily Ulster descent, and Washington said: "If defeated everywhere else I will make my last stand for liberty among the Scotch-Irish of my native Virginia."

The Official Declaration of Independence was written in the handwriting of Charles Thompson from Maghera, printed by John Dunlap from Strabane, given its first public reading by the son of an Ulsterman, Colonel John Nixon, and the Scots-Irish were well represented among the signatories.

Ten United States Presidents have been of direct Ulster descent: Andrew Jackson, James Knox Polk, James Buchanan, Andrew Johnson, Ulysses S Grant, Chester Alan Arthur, Grover Cleveland, Benjamin Harrison, William McKinley and Woodrow Wilson.

The radicalism fostered in America soon found its way back to Ireland, especially among progressive Presbyterians in Belfast, where it proved a potent stimulus to the founding of the Society of United Irishmen, the aim of which was "to form a brotherhood of affection among Irishmen of every religious persuasion", and whose attempt to create an independent Ireland led to the ill-fated rebellion of 1798.

Although the Scots-Irish eventually merged into the American nation, Ulster speech itself was to stay alive in the hill-country of Appalachia and beyond, where Scots-Irish traditional music may still be heard. Rooted deep in the traditions of the British Isles peasantry, the fiddle had become an instrument of major importance in the development of Irish, Scottish and Welsh jigs, reels and hornpipes. Transposed to America, the hoe-down fiddle reached the peak of its development in the Southern States. Musicologist W H Williams has written:

Ireland's initial impact upon American music came predominantly from Ulster... Whatever their influence in terms of cabin and barn styles, field layout, town planning, and so on, it seems likely that the greatest and most lasting contribution of the Scotch-Irish was music. And however one may define their particular religious and ethnic identity, musically they should be considered Ulstermen, for they brought with them the mixture of Scottish and Irish tunes which is still characteristic of large parts of Northern Ireland. When the great English folklorist Cecil Sharp went into the Appalachians to rediscover 'English' folk song, he was in fact often dealing with people of Ulster descent. Wherever they settled in large numbers and remained in relative isolation, balladry has been found 'live and in a healthy condition'. [33]

As the authors of *The Story of English* inform us:

Their rhymes and ditties came from the traditions of Scotland and Ireland. Their ballads, such as *Edward*, tell the stories of their ancestors, and the tunes of the Scottish Lowland ballads of the sixteenth and seventeenth centuries have been an important influence in the making of American country music. Today the ballads of the Scots-Irish... are imitated and reproduced from Arkansas to Alberta, by singers like Dolly Parton and Kenny Rodgers who have internationalised a style that was once confined to the hills. [34]

The American Civil War of 1861-1865 produced some prominent military leaders on both sides who had Ulster-Scots or Irish lineage. Names like Ulysses Simpson Grant, Commander-in-Chief of the Union Army; General Philip Henry Sheridan, the cavalry commander who outmanoeuvred Confederate Commander-in-Chief Robert E. Lee and forced him to surrender at Appomatax; General George B McClelland, the soldier of greatest reputation in the North for a considerable part of the war; Thomas 'Stonewall' Jackson, the outstanding Confederate

General; and the only man victorious against the latter, General James Shields.

General Robert E Lee was once asked "what race makes the best soldiers?" To which the General answered: "The Scotch who came to this country by way of Ireland... Because they have all the dash of the Irish in taking a position, and all the stubbornness of the Scotch in holding it."

A New Awareness of our Shared Heritage

I hope that the episodes explored in this pamphlet lend support to my assertion that the heritage of the Ulster people is very much an *interrelated* one. If some of the history is new to the reader, I hope it stimulates earnest reflection on the reality of our tragic communal divide. If, on the other hand, it is already well known, I hope that it serves to reinforce what must be readily acknowledged – that the peoples of Ireland and Scotland share a unique heritage and an ancient kinship, and therefore the people of Ulster have much more in common with each other than they might presently realise.

Sources:

1   Dr Patrick Hillery, speech to United Nations Security Council, 1969.

2   Estyn Evans, *The Personality of Ireland*, Blackstaff Press, Belfast, 1981.

3   W C Mackenzie, *The Races of Ireland and Scotland*, Alexander Gardner.

4   Peter C Woodman, *The Mesolithic in Ireland*, British Archaeological Report 58, 1978.

5   Séan P O Ríordáin, *Antiquities of the Irish Countryside*, Methuen, 1973.

6   J P Mallory and T E McNeill, *The Archaeology of Ulster*, The Institute of Irish Studies, Queen's University, Belfast, 1991

7   Peter Woodman, 'Prehistoric Settlers', *The People of Ireland*, edited by Patrick Loughrey, Appletree Press/BBC, 1988.

8   Liam de Paor, 'The People of Ireland', *The People of Ireland*, edited by Patrick Loughrey, Appletree Press/BBC, Belfast, 1988.

9   Ian Adamson, *The Ulster People*, Pretani Press, Belfast, 1991.

10 Francis J Byrne, 'Early Irish Society', *The Course of Irish History*, Mercier/RTE, Cork, 1984.

11 Charles Doherty, 'Ulster before the Normans: ancient myth and early history,' *Ulster: An Illustrated History*, Batsford, London, 1989.

12 Thomas L Markey, 'The Language of Stonehenge', *L.S.A.*, Unversity of Michigan, 1988.

13 Francis J Byrne, *Irish Kings and High Kings*, Batsford, London, 1973.

14 Liam de Paor, 'Roots', *Irish Times*, 15 July 1975.

15 T F O'Rahilly, *Early Irish History and Mythology*, Dublin Institute for Advanced Studies, 1984.

16 Shirley Toulson, *Celtic Journeys*, Hutchinson, London, 1985.

17 'Scotland; History', *Encyclopaedia Britannica* (Ninth Edition), 1886.

18 Eleanor Hull, *Pagan Ireland*, David Nutt, 1904.

19 Proinsias Mac Cana, 'Mongán Mac Fiachna and *Immram Brain*', in *Eriu*, vol. XXIII, Dublin, 1972.

20 Douglas Hyde, *A Literary History of Ireland*, T Fisher Unwin, London, 1906.

21 Thomas Kinsella, *The Táin*, Dolmen Press/Oxford University Press, Dublin, 1983.

22 Charles Thomas, *Britain and Ireland in Early Christian Times*, Thames and Hudson, London, 1984.

23 Edmund Curtis, *A History of Ireland*, Methuen, 1970.

24 Denis Kennedy, Foreword to T M Healy, *The Great Fraud of Ulster*, Tralee, 1971.

25 Rev George Hill, *An Historical Account of the Plantation in Ulster at the Commencement of the Seventeenth Century 1608–1620*, Belfast, 1877.

26 P L Henry, *Ulster Dialects*, Ulster Folk Museum, 1964.

27 F J Bigger, 'From Uladh to Galloway and From Galloway to Uladh', *The Red Hand Magazine*, vol 1 no 3, November 1920.

28 A T Q Stewart, *The Narrow Ground*, Pretani Press, Belfast, 1986.

29 Ian Adamson, *The Identity of Ulster*, Pretani Press, Belfast, 1981.

30 Ulick O'Connor, introduction to *Skylark sing your lonely song*, Bobby Sands, Mercier Press, 1982.

31 E Wright, in *The Ulster-American Connection*, The New University of Ulster, 1981.

32 James G Leyburn, *The Scotch-Irish: A Social History*, University of North Carolina Press, 1962.

33 W H A Williams, 'Irish Traditional Music in the United States', *America and Ireland: 1776–1976*, Greenwood Press, USA, 1980.

34 Robert McCrum, William Cran and Robert MacNeil, *The Story of English*, Faber and Faber/BBC, London, 1986.